FISHING S[

Carp Fishing

Tony Whieldon

Introduction by Jim Gibbinson

WARD LOCK

© Ward Lock Limited 1987

First published in Great Britain in 1987
by Ward Lock Limited, Villiers House,
41–47 Strand, London, WC2N 5JE,
a Cassell Company.

Printed and bound in the UK by Bath Press

British Library Cataloguing in Publication Data

Whieldon, Tony
  Carp fishing.——(Fishing skills)
  1. Carp fishing——Great Britain
  I. Title   II. Series
  799.1′752   SH691.C3

ISBN 0-7063-6446-5

Reprinted 1990, 1991

Contents

Acknowledgments

With thanks to my son Michael for
his assistance.

Introduction

Carp are special. No other fish produces among its devotees such obsessive single-mindedness. Carp fishing is, to many of its adherents, the most important thing in life; more important than job, home and health.

The appeal of carp is easy to understand – they are big, powerful and, where they grow large, difficult to tempt. The capture of any carp, whatever its size, feels like a special achievement, whilst the capture of a big one produces a sense of elation, euphoria even, that only another carp angler can possibly understand. This is by no means a new phenomenon as was witnessed by the late Edward Marston who, writing in the now defunct *Fishing Gazette* some thirty or more years ago said, "I have respectfully shaken hands with the man who caught the largest carp in England, he looked as though he had been in Heaven and Hell and had nothing else to live for".

In Marston's day the British record was held by a 26½ lb (12 kg) carp captured by Albert Buckley from Mapperly Reservoir – the current record is almost double that weight! Its precise weight was 51 lb 6 oz (23.5 kg) and it was caught by Chris Yates in June 1980 from Redmire Pool, the same water that produced the fish it deposed, Richard Walker's 44-pounder (20 kg). In the interests of accuracy I ought to mention that the 51-pounder (23 kg) is not recognized by the British Record Fish Committee (BRFC), who disallowed it on a technicality, but it is recognized by the National Association of Specialist Anglers' (NASA) Record Committee and by the vast majority of carp anglers.

However, only a small proportion of carp anglers will ever see a fish of 30 lb (13.5 kg), which is why the dreams and ambitions of most carp anglers revolve around the capture of their first 20-pounder (9 kg). The simple truth is that most carp waters just don't hold 20-pounders (9 kg), and even those that do rarely hold more than one or two. The newcomer to carp fishing reading the angling press could be forgiven for thinking that carp anglers up and down the country are constantly whipping the water to a froth pulling out such fish! It isn't the case. There are many capable carp anglers who have yet to catch their first 'twenty'.

Not surprisingly, the waters that are known to hold a reasonable number of 20-pounders (9 kg) are very popular and tend to be crowded throughout the summer and autumn, and are fished steadily even through the winter. Carp in these waters have 'seen it all' so new methods and baits have had to be devised to outwit them. Carp anglers are an inventive lot and the last few seasons have been something of a renaissance, with totally new approaches being developed. Inevitably snippets of information about these new methods 'leaked out', with the result that carp fishing has undergone greater change than any other sort of fishing. Things have moved so rapidly that a friend of mine who dropped out of carp fishing three or four years ago has been discouraged from taking it up again because he feels hopelessly out of touch with recent developments. He said, "I bought an angling magazine and read the articles on carp fishing – and do you know, I couldn't understand half of what was written".

That comment was made by a man who until a few seasons ago was very successful, with numerous 20-pounders (9 kg) to his credit . . . so what of the poor newcomer? How does the beginner make sense of the esoteric language and begin to understand the complexities of this, the most specialized of all branches of fishing? Well he (or she) has made a good start by reading this book, which cuts through a lot of the mystique and explains things in a clear, easy-to-understand manner. Angling in general lends itself particularly well to instruction via the medium of pictures, and carp fishing is no exception.

Having read the book and acquired the sometimes specialized items of equipment that are necessary, the newcomer should choose their first carp water with great care. I have no hesitation in recommending that the beginner steer well clear of the well known big-fish waters, for the moment anyway. Far better to choose the sort of water that the big-fish specialists ignore, where the carp are plentiful but not very large. The ideal water would hold lots of carp in the 5-10 lb (2.2-4.5 kg) range – big enough to give the flavour and excitement of carp fishing but not so intimidating or difficult as to be likely to result in a long succession of unsuccessful outings. A beginner needs success and will learn very little from failure. So lower your sights, forget about 20-pounders (9 kg) and concentrate on acquiring a sound base of experience.

Choice of a suitable water will be relatively easy if you live in the southern half of the country (with the exception of Devon and Cornwall where carp are relatively scarce). Even in the Midlands it shouldn't be too difficult, but if you live in the North you'll almost certainly be denied the luxury of choice. North of Yorkshire, carp waters are scarce.

Most carp waters are in the hands of clubs and associations which can be joined for between £10 and £15 per year. Many of those reading this book will already be members of clubs that own or control the fishing on a number of carp waters. The lack of suitable clubs need not be a barrier, however, because there are a lot of very productive waters that can be fished on a day-ticket, whilst commercial angling clubs such as Leisure Sport (which can be joined by anyone, there being no geographical restrictions) own some of the best carp waters in the country.

Some carp anglers are natural loners and like to 'do their thing' in solitude – others are somewhat gregarious and enjoy the social side of carp fishing, especially informal get-togethers. All will benefit from membership of either the Carp Anglers' Association (CAA) or the Carp Society. Both organizations publish top-quality magazines that are issued free to members. They also organize national and regional meetings where you can listen to talks by well-known carp anglers, or simply chat about the sport with like-minded enthusiasts.

The carp is a magnificent animal. Our pursuit of this, the most cunning of all freshwater fish, takes us to some beautiful places – let us remember always to treat the carp and its environment with the respect they both deserve.

Jim Gibbinson
Cuxton, Kent.

January 1986.

Carp

COMMON CARP

Carp have been bred
selectively in Europe since
the Roman era, and as a
result there now exist
three main varieties.

COMMON CARP are covered
with a uniform layer of scales.

MIRROR CARP have larger
and more irregular scaling.

LEATHER CARP are almost
scaleless.

WILD CARP are more
streamlined in the body
and do not grow to the
proportions of the cultivated
varieties, but are much
faster swimmers.

Carp can grow to a weight
of 50 lb (23 kg) in Britain
and weights closer to 100 lb
(45 kg) are possible in some
parts of Europe.

MIRROR CARP

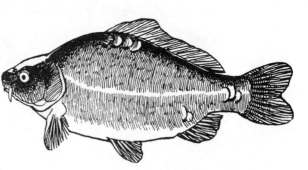

LEATHER CARP

WILD CARP

Carp waters

Carp seem to thrive best in lowland lakes and ponds which are partially surrounded by trees and contain a rich growth of weed on which, to some extent, they feed. Other items of food consist of water fleas, bloodworms, snails, nymphs and larvae, water bugs and fresh-water mussels. Many of the man-made lakes, which were constructed during the early nineteenth century on country estates and parkland, usually possess these features and often contain carp. These lakes are often fairly sheltered from the wind, which is another point in their favour.

Unlikely-looking waters are also worth investigating. One I know in particular is no larger than half an acre, and was created when a farmer did a small excavation, and made a dam of clay on the course of a small farm-land stream.

Flooded gravel pits can provide ideal habitats for carp. Some are already established as Fisheries and many more are on the way. Although, at first sight, the geography of a pit can appear rather featureless, the contours below the surface are quite the opposite. Submerged plateaux, shelves and ledges make ideal feeding areas for carp.
(More information on this subject can be found in 'Modern Specimen Hunting', by Jim Gibbinson.)

Carp have also been introduced into some canals with excellent results.

On occasions, good catches of carp are taken from the slower reaches of certain rivers, for example, The Trent and The Thames.

Some flooded quarries also have their quota of carp. These places are often surrounded by precipitous, overgrown banks which provide a challenge to the angler and a haven for the fish.

Carp behaviour

Carp are predominantly bottom feeders, and in the process of doing so often betray their activities by creating bubbles which surge to the surface.

If the water is shallow and the bottom muddy, areas of water will become cloudy with all the rooting activity below. If more than one carp is feeding, large areas of water will soon become cloudy with muddy suspension.

Early mornings and evenings are common feeding times, when it is not unusual to see them feeding only inches from the bank.

During hot, sunny weather carp can often be seen cruising just beneath the surface....

.... or just basking.

Whatever the weather they can always be found lying beneath trees that have fallen into the water.

13

During mild, overcast weather carp will feed throughout the day. If a warm south or south-west wind is blowing across the lake carp will congregate along the windward shore, especially if the water is shallower there.

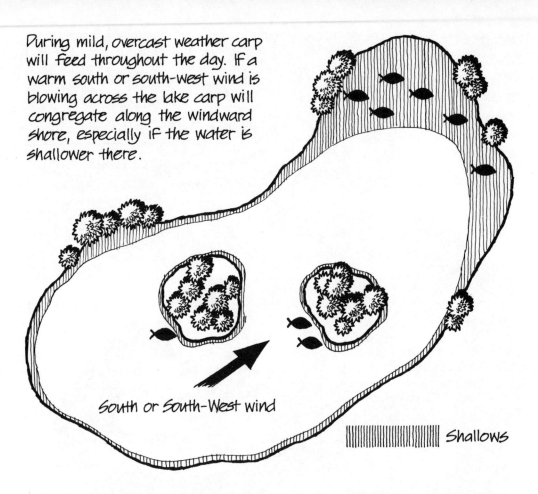

South or South-West wind

|||||||||||||||||||||||||||||| Shallows

Shallow areas found in the middle of some waters will also attract carp during these weather conditions. It is an advantage, therefore, that the angler is well conversant with the underwater topography of the carp water that he intends to fish.

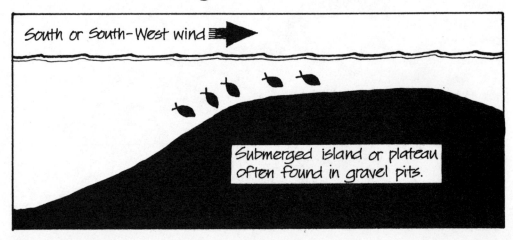

South or South-West wind ➡

Submerged island or plateau often found in gravel pits.

Carp tackle

No angler can possibly hope for consistent success with these powerful fish without a rod which meets the necessary requirements. Large carp have, it is true, been landed on match rods, light leger rods and even fly rods, but to approach carp fishing permanently armed with one of these flimsy affairs would be an act of the utmost temerity.

Fibreglass and carbon-fibre rods can be purchased in a ready-made form or as a blank, the fittings being bought separately and attached by the angler. The latter method is, of course, considerably cheaper.

The rings of a carp rod are subjected to an enormous amount of friction when a heavy fish is being played. Inadequate rings will quickly develop grooves, create an abrasion point, and have disastrous effects on the line. Titania-alumina oxide and silicon carbide are both excellent ring materials and will never wear out.

Carp rods are usually between 10ft (3.05m) and 11ft (3.35m) in length with a 30in (75cm) handle.

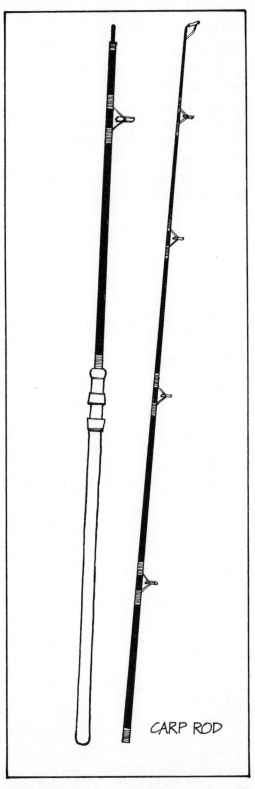

CARP ROD

Carp rods usually have a test curve of about 1½ lb (0·70 kg)

This test rating was formulated by Richard Walker in the 1950s, when he was in the process of designing a built cane rod suitable for catching big carp. This rod ultimately came to be known as the Mk IV.

Some carp specialists still use this model even today.

The Walker test rating is still used as a yard-stick for glass and carbon rods, although heavier models with 2lb (0·90kg) test curves are also used for coping with long casts and heavily weeded waters, where stronger lines are needed.

It pays to apply the test curve idea when playing a large fish. Do this by holding the rod at such an angle to the direction of the line that it is being employed most efficiently.

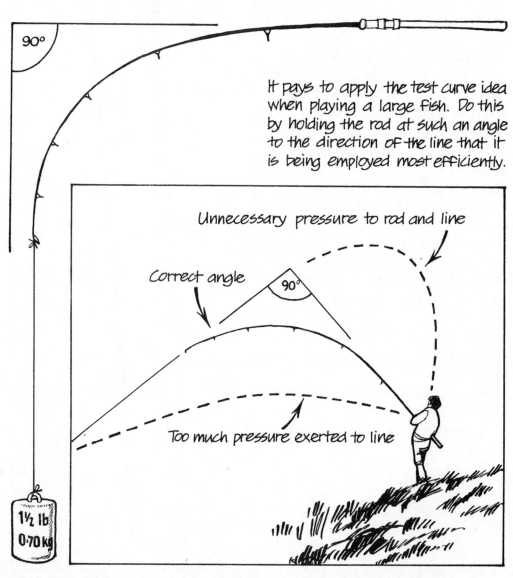

90°

Unnecessary pressure to rod and line

Correct angle

90°

Too much pressure exerted to line

1½ lb
0·70 kg

The reel

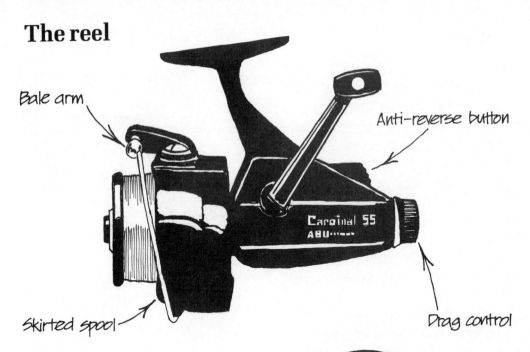

Bale arm

Anti-reverse button

Cardinal 55
ABU

Skirted spool

Drag control

The reel shown above contains all the features necessary for trouble-free carp fishing. The skirted spool mitigates the problem of line fouling the internal mechanism; the bale arm return springing is positive and robust; and finally the drag control and anti-reverse button are easily accessible.

A line of 8lb (3·50 kg) to 9lb (4·00kg) test is adequate for swims which contain little or no weed, but heavier monofilament line of 11lb (5·00 kg) to 12 lb (5·50 kg) will be necessary in heavily weeded areas or where snags are known to exist. Featured opposite are just a few of the many brands of quality monofilament line now available.

Hooks

The main requirement of a carp hook is that it should be strong. It therefore follows that the forged variety, which are renowned for their robustness, are the ideal choice. Sizes 4, 6 and 8, in bronze and gold will meet most requirements depending on what bait is being used. For example, if sweetcorn is the bait a size 8 gold would be the most logical choice as the colour of the bait is also golden.

My favourite pattern is the 'Sundridge Specimen'. It has a wide gape, sharp point, a neat, short shank and a straight eye. One warning, however, even with top-quality hooks: always check each one before use. The most common fault with eyed hooks is that the eye has not been properly completed; a squeeze with a pair of pliers will remedy this.

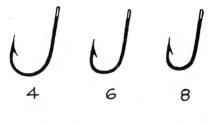

4   6   8

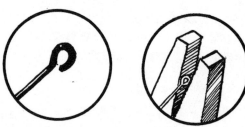

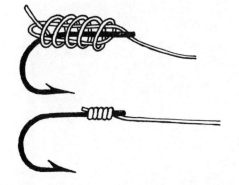

The standard whip finish type of knot is best for hook connection as it holds the hook rigid and prevents a hinging action. In my experience, the line is best threaded through the eye on the <u>inside</u> of the hook.

Bite indicators

The variety of bite indicators now being put to use for signalling carp bites is so vast that it would be possible to devote a whole volume to the subject. However, I believe that the approach to carp fishing should be kept as simple as possible. These are my favourites.

PEACOCK QUILL FLOATING INDICATOR (For use at close-range in shallow water).

This is literally a length of peacock quill about 6in (15 cm) long, held to the line by a float or valve rubber at each end.

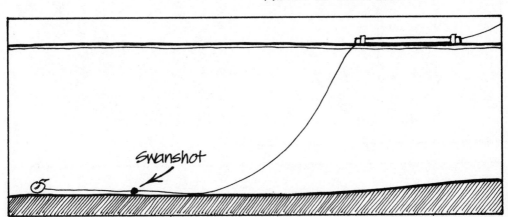

Swanshot

When using a particle bait such as sweetcorn some additional weight may be needed to assist casting. If this weight is enough to cause the carp to eject the hookbait (signalled by the float jerking forwards and then lying still) the weight is best fixed at each end of the quill.

Lead wire

Lead wire

MONKEY CLIMB

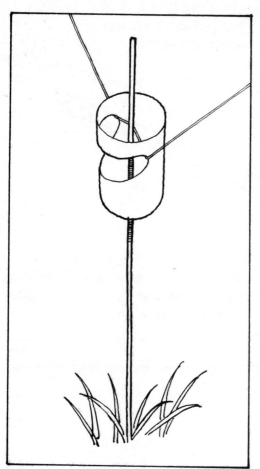

A handy little gadget, which can be made in a variety of sizes by utilizing other objects like rigid plastic tubing, bottle caps and such like. The stainless steel or alloy needle keeps the 'monkey' stable during a wind and also locks it on to the needle until a strike is made, when the 'monkey' comes free. There are many variations on this theme and some shop-bought ones have a built-in isotope for fishing at night.

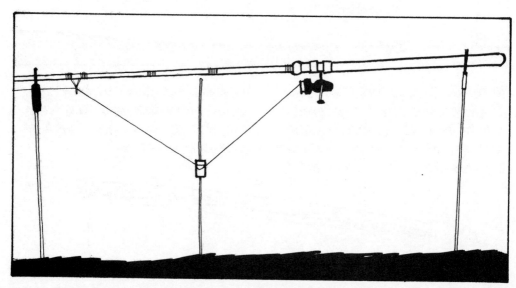

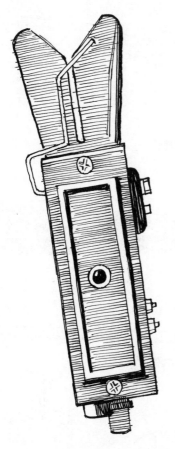

Del Romang 'Heron'

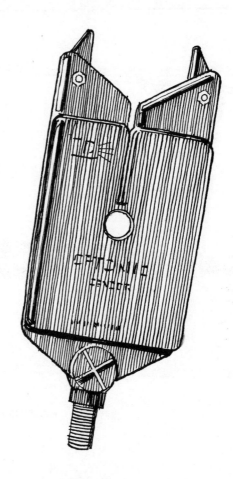

'Optonic'

The Del Romang 'Heron' is activated by pressure on the line which moves the antenna. The Optonic has a special wheel over which the line runs. Both types emit a bleep tone and have a light emitting diode (LED). They are invaluable for the night angler.

Bite alarms can be attached to any standard bank stick by means of the built-in screw thread.

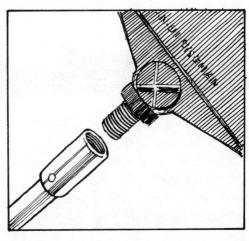

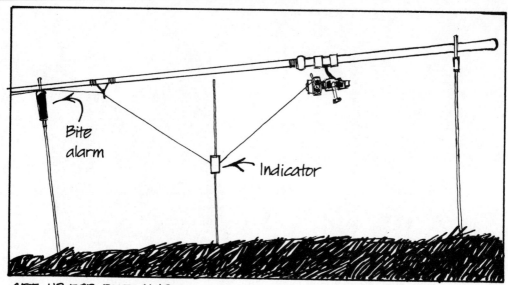

SET-UP FOR BITE ALARM

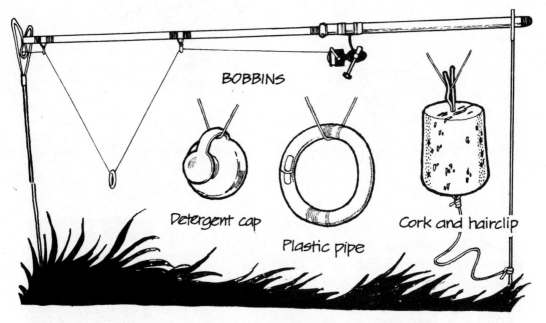

BOBBINS

Detergent cap

Plastic pipe

Cork and hairclip

Here are a few more simple and effective ideas for bite indication. It is important that the detergent cap and plastic pipe indicators are suspended between the butt ring and the ring above it in order to avoid tangling up with the reel.
The cork and clip indicator can be used between the butt ring and the reel because it is pulled free of the line when the rod is lifted.

LANDING NET

A special mention must be made of this very important item of carping equipment. It must, of course, be very large, having arms of at least 36in(90cm) in length and a depth of about 48in(120cm). The handle needs to be at least 5ft(1·50m) long.

Baits

BREAD CRUST : A very versatile bait which can be used floating on the surface, resting on a submerged weedbed or floating just off the bottom.

BREAD PASTE : Using clean hands, a sticky paste is made by mixing the centre part of the loaf with water. To drain any excess moisture, put the paste in a clean tea towel and squeeze. A further kneading with the hands is then necessary to produce the right consistency.

Line lies along bottom

Bread paste can also be used in conjunction with crust. If the correct amount of paste is moulded around the shank of the hook it will cause the crust to sink very slowly, coming to rest on soft mud or silkweed without sinking into it.

Bread paste can be flavoured with many things, honey being one of the all-time favourites. Experiments are worthwhile with trout pellets (which of course must be dissolved before mixing with the bread paste), fish paste, cheese and vanilla.
Bread paste is best mixed at home and transported to the waterside wrapped in damp muslin or cloth.

LOBWORM: Definitely a big fish bait. They can be collected from lawns on a mild night when the ground is damp. A torch is necessary for this operation to illuminate the worm as it lies outside its hole. A stealthy approach is also required as any vibration will send the worm retreating in a flash.

Tail

REDWORM: 'If I was restricted to just one carp bait for the rest of my fishing career it would be redworms.' (Jim Gibbinson – 'Modern Specimen Hunting').
A very logical statement, for a lively redworm is probably the closest thing to resemble one of the carp's chief natural food items – the bloodworm. If a bunch of very small redworms are presented as bait it must be irresistible to a feeding carp.

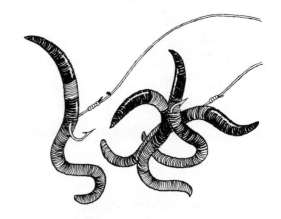

BRANDLING: This is not a very pleasant worm to use as hook-bait, but it can be used very effectively as a free offering to encourage carp to feed in an area where redworms are being used as hookbait. They can be collected by the score from manure heaps.

LUNCHEON MEAT AND SAUSAGE

Effective and convenient baits which can be carried in the tackle bag and made ready for use by a few turns of a tin opener. A blotting paper support may be needed when long casts are made, as these baits tend to fly off the hook in mid air.

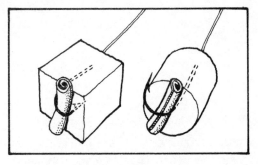

TINNED POTATOES: Another bait which can be carried at all times in the tackle bag, and extracted for instant use. Potatoes and the two baits above are best mounted on the hook by threading the line through the bait with a baiting needle, then attaching the hook and pulling it back into the bait.

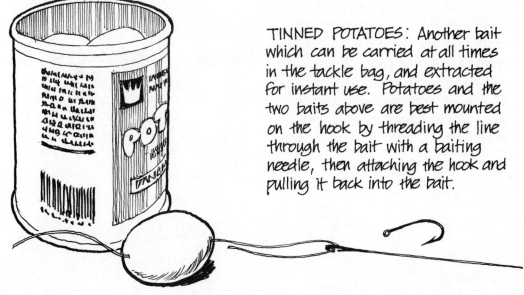

SWEETCORN : An excellent and convenient bait. However the pre-cooked, tinned variety can be expensive if used for loose feed as well as hook bait. By purchasing loose maize from your local corn merchant this can be cooked and used as loose feed, while the larger, tinned variety can be used on the hook. This procedure will reduce the cost dramatically over the season.

BEANS : Butter beans and black eyed beans can be purchased loose from all health food shops, and when cooked provide a good alternative bait. However, the true value as bait lies in the fact that these particles can be purchased, ready cooked, in tins. If a tin is kept in the tackle bag as a contingency bait it can be withdrawn for service immediately.

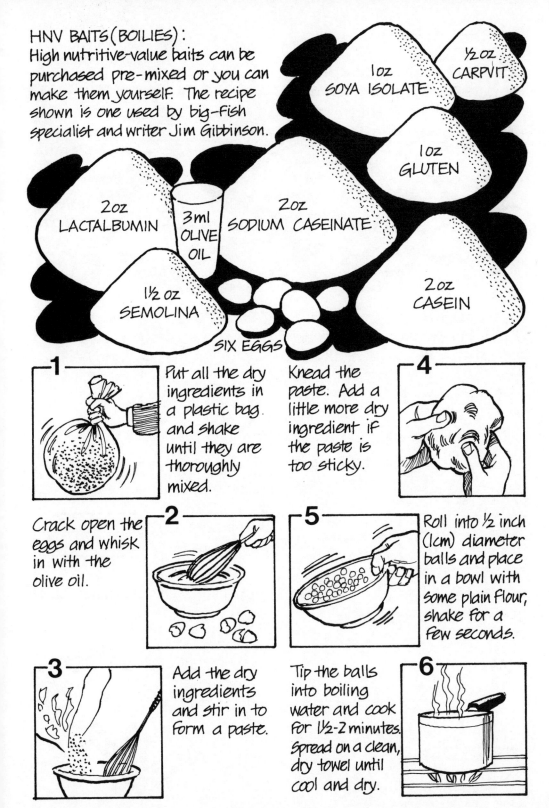

HNV BAITS (BOILIES):
High nutritive-value baits can be purchased pre-mixed or you can make them yourself. The recipe shown is one used by big-fish specialist and writer Jim Gibbinson.

1oz SOYA ISOLATE

½oz CARPVIT

1oz GLUTEN

2oz LACTALBUMIN

3ml OLIVE OIL

2oz SODIUM CASEINATE

1½oz SEMOLINA

SIX EGGS

2oz CASEIN

1 Put all the dry ingredients in a plastic bag and shake until they are thoroughly mixed.

Knead the paste. Add a little more dry ingredient if the paste is too sticky.

4

Crack open the eggs and whisk in with the olive oil.

2

5

Roll into ½ inch (1cm) diameter balls and place in a bowl with some plain flour; shake for a few seconds.

3

Add the dry ingredients and stir in to form a paste.

Tip the balls into boiling water and cook for 1½-2 minutes. Spread on a clean, dry towel until cool and dry.

6

FLOATER: Breadcrust was the original floating bait and still is very effective in waters that are not overfished. However, the carp angler can often maintain more consistent success by producing an alternative.

1oz SOYA ISOLATE

1oz GLUTEN

2oz CASEIN

1 TEASPOONFUL OF CARPVIT

2oz SODIUM CASEINATE

2oz SEMOLINA

2oz LACTALBUMIN

1 LEVEL TEASPOONFUL OF BAKING POWDER.

1 DOZEN EGGS

This is another recipe used by Jim Gibbinson and the ingredients are virtually the same as those used for the HNV bait, but in this case the baking powder replaces the olive oil.

1

Put all the dry ingredients in a plastic bag and shake until they are thoroughly mixed.

Stir the dry mix in with 1 dozen beaten eggs.

2

3

Flavouring can be added at this stage, if required.

4

Pour the mixture into a lightly oiled non-stick bread tin.

Place in a preheated oven at gas Mk 2 or electric 300 for 1½-2 hours.

5

6

After cooking knock the Floater on to a wire grid and leave to cool.

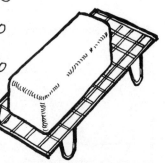

Floater can be fished on the surface.....

..... near the bottom.... .... or at any depth.

MUNCHIES: This cat food makes a convenient floater bait, but is too hard for the hook to penetrate until it has been soaked for some time.

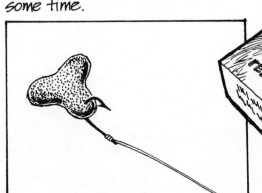 

Terminal tackle

FREELINE

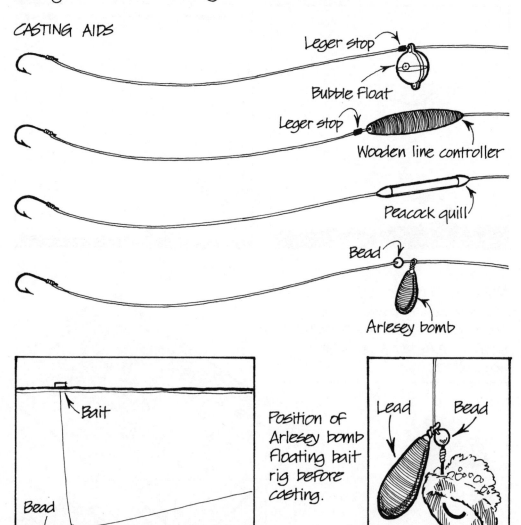

This rig comprises solely of the hook, line and bait. The bait, however, must have enough weight in itself to make any sort of a cast practical, (breadcrust and luncheon meat are ideal).
The line needs to be as fine as possible, depending on the nature of the swim.

In order to cast a small, floating bait any distance some sort of casting aid will be necessary.

CASTING AIDS

Leger stop

Bubble float

Leger stop

Wooden line controller

Peacock quill

Bead

Arlesey bomb

Bait

Bead

Bomb

Position of Arlesey bomb floating bait rig before casting.

Lead   Bead

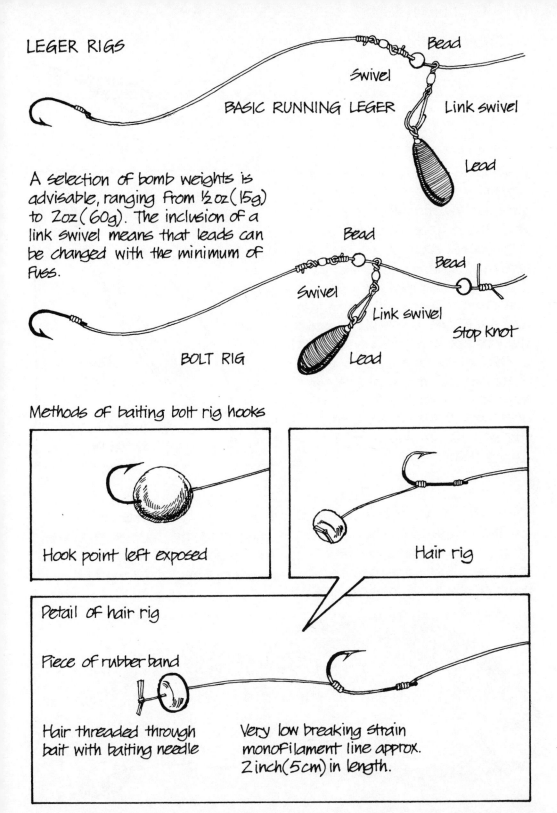

LEGER RIGS

BASIC RUNNING LEGER

Bead

Swivel

Link swivel

Lead

A selection of bomb weights is advisable, ranging from ½oz(15g) to 2oz(60g). The inclusion of a link swivel means that leads can be changed with the minimum of fuss.

BOLT RIG

Bead

Bead

Swivel

Link swivel

Lead

Stop knot

Methods of baiting bolt rig hooks

Hook point left exposed

Hair rig

Detail of hair rig

Piece of rubber band

Hair threaded through bait with baiting needle

Very low breaking strain monofilament line approx. 2 inch(5cm) in length.

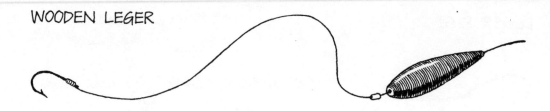

By shaping a piece of hardwood dowelling to the shape of a torpedo and attaching a strip of lead, the carp angler will have a very useful casting aid and neutral buoyancy leger weight. Trial and error testing in a container of water will show just how much lead is needed to make the wood sink very slowly. The lead is then stuck to the wood with 'Araldite' and the whole thing painted in a drab colour. The advantage of this weight is that it presents no resistance to a taking fish.

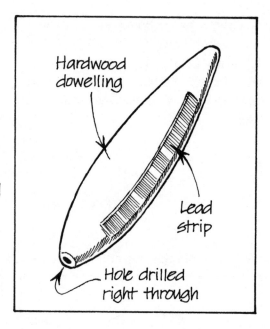

Hardwood dowelling

Lead strip

Hole drilled right through

The bolt rig, which was designed for the downfall of shy-biting carp, works on the opposite principle. The carp feels the point of the hook, panics, and tries to eject the bait and in so doing pulls the back-stop against the weight of the lead. The result is a very fast, blistering run.

Groundbaiting

Groundbait is best introduced in an area where carp are known to feed or visit naturally and regularly, or in an area where the bottom contours of the lake provide features which interest the fish. (Anywhere on a patrol route is worth baiting).

◖ Good groundbait areas.

– – – – – Patrol routes.

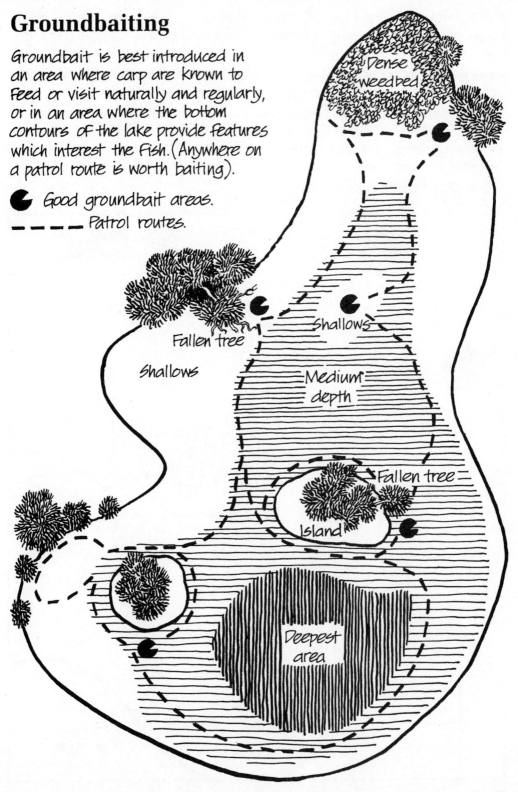

Dense weedbed

Fallen tree

Shallows

Shallows

Medium depth

Fallen tree

Island

Deepest area

Pre-baiting with a mixture of brown bread crumb and hookbait samples over a period of three or four days before the actual fishing day will have the best effect. On the fishing day just hookbait samples will suffice. Accurate delivery of groundbait and baited hook is of great importance.

When groundbaiting at medium or long range, features on the far bank or beyond can be used to ensure that the groundbait and hookbait fall within the desired area. If two rods are being used it is best to have the baits fishing in two different areas, therefore two areas will have to be groundbaited.

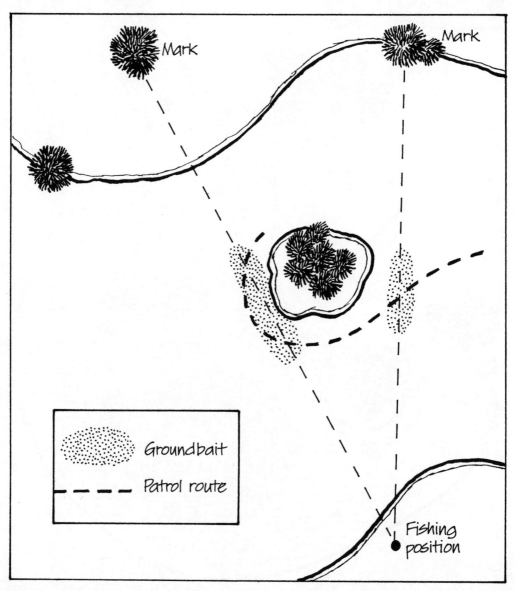

Mark

Mark

Groundbait

Patrol route

Fishing position

Groundbaiting at fairly close range
can be done by hand.

For longer range work a catapult
will have to be brought into use.

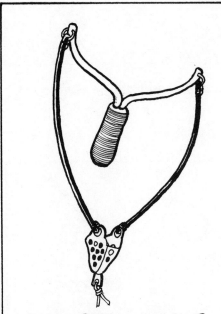

Loose feed catapult for
introducing small
hookbait particles.

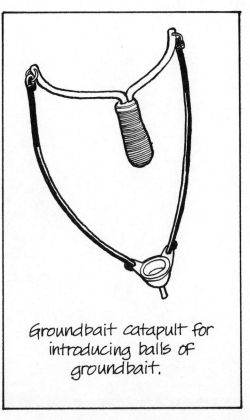

Groundbait catapult for
introducing balls of
groundbait.

Crucian carp

Before moving on to big carp tactics, a mention must be made of the little CRUCIAN CARP, which seldom grows much above 3lb (1·35kg), and can be caught on roach-type tackle. This fish can be identified by the lack of barbules around the mouth.

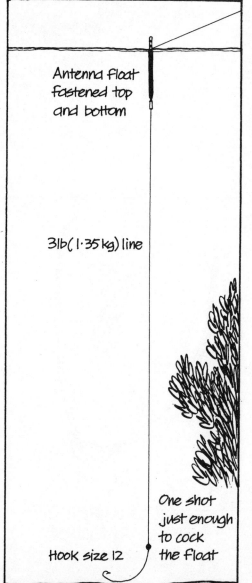

Antenna float fastened top and bottom

3lb (1·35kg) line

Hook size 12

One shot just enough to cock the float

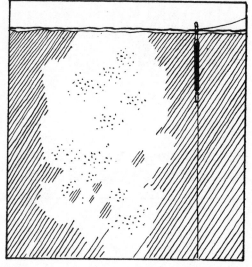

Cloud groundbait as for roach.

BAITS

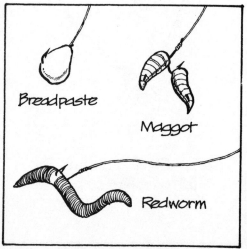

Breadpaste

Maggot

Redworm

Stalking a carp

Carp have good eyesight and are very sensitive to bankside vibrations. The angler, therefore, needs to keep a very low profile, making use of whatever cover is available to screen his approach. Dress should be drab in colour—ex-government battle dress is perfect.

Soft-soled desert boots make ideal footwear if conditions permit, but quite often carp lakes are fringed with boggy areas, where lightweight rubber boots are more suitable. If waders must be worn avoid the ones with studs in the soles.

Carp like to swim around the
marginal shallows in twos and
threes. At certain points they
will put their heads down and
grub around on the bottom before
continuing their patrol.

The angler can take advantage
of this feeding behaviour by
stalking to a point ahead of the
carp in preparation for an
ambush.

Free offerings with the
baited hook cast into
their midst. Sweetcorn
is ideal for this approach.

This close range ambush fishing can be done with a freelined rig or with a length of peacock quill on the line. Whatever method is used the angler usually has only one chance of success before the carp move on or are spooked.

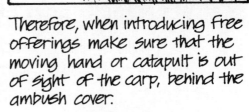

Therefore, when introducing free offerings make sure that the moving hand or catapult is out of sight of the carp, behind the ambush cover.

Also keep the rod tip tucked into the bank as close to cover as possible.

Do not attempt to strike at every little twitch on the line or quill but wait for a positive, steady movement.

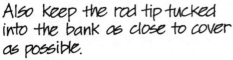

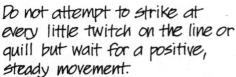

Fishing a floater

Floating baits can be most productive in areas where carp are visibly active on or near the surface, usually in or around lily or weed beds. When fishing in such areas it is a sensible precaution to use line of about 11lb (5kg) breaking strain.

The line should also be treated with a line floatant to ensure that it rides high-and-dry on the surface.

If bread crust is the chosen bait its attraction will be enhanced by leaving a good amount of the centre of the loaf attached to the crust. A sharp penknife can be used to cut a suitably sized bait direct from the loaf as and when it is needed.

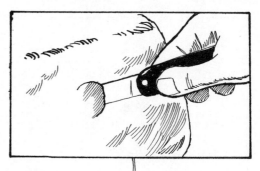

The excess crumb hanging beneath the surface will provide an attractive stimulant for the carp, especially if loose particles are sinking from the bait.

Freelined bread crust needs to be cut to a size which will provide enough casting weight. It must also be large enough to survive the ravages of small fish.

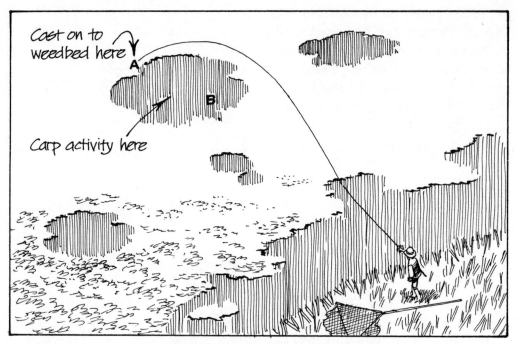

Cast on to
weedbed here

A

B

Carp activity here

If bread crust is being used, a very quick, single dunk in the margins will supply that extra bit of weight to make casting easier.

After the cast has been made the bait should be retrieved very slowly, without a ripple, to come to rest at point B.

The line is now hidden from the carp's viewpoint and runs back across the supporting weeds. Prior to fishing, it is often good

policy to throw in a few free crusts, which should be identical in size to the crust being used as hook bait.

Carp frequently have the annoying habit of playing with a floating crust without actually taking it into their mouths. This applies especially on hard-fished waters.

This problem can often be solved by threading an extra large crust just up the line from the hook, which is baited with a small crust. This gives the impression that the smaller crust has broken away from the larger crust, and it is usually taken very confidently.

Fishing in weedy areas with a floating bait calls for absolute vigilance. A carp can suck in a bait, move away and eject it all within the space of a few seconds, very seldom returning for a second helping.

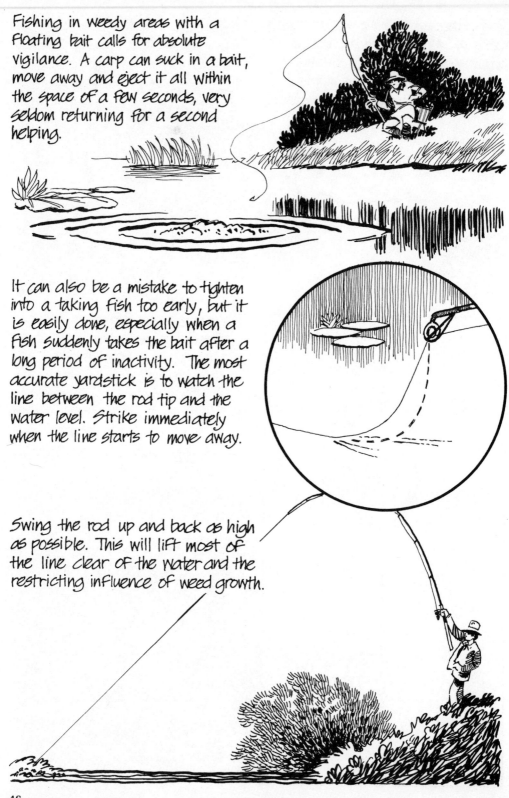

It can also be a mistake to tighten into a taking fish too early, but it is easily done, especially when a fish suddenly takes the bait after a long period of inactivity. The most accurate yardstick is to watch the line between the rod tip and the water level. Strike immediately when the line starts to move away.

Swing the rod up and back as high as possible. This will lift most of the line clear of the water and the restricting influence of weed growth.

If a hooked carp dives into dense weed and refuses to move, no amount of rod pressure will bring it out. If, however, the rod is lowered, thus creating slack line the fish will invariably come free. The rod should then be immediately raised to its former position.

A certain amount of bullying is advisable when playing a carp in and around weed. If possible the carp should be played into a clear area (if one exists) and brought to the net without undue delay.

When fishing in weedy areas it is a good idea to have an experienced companion present whose assistance will be invaluable.

The distance at which a floating bait can be cast with the freeline method is limited, therefore extra weight has to be supplied in order to produce longer casts.

The home-made floater bait would be best for the job as bread crust may have a tendency to fly off the hook during the force of the cast.

This rig is ideal for far bank or island drop offs, where the depth does not exceed 5 or 6ft (1·50 or 1·85m).

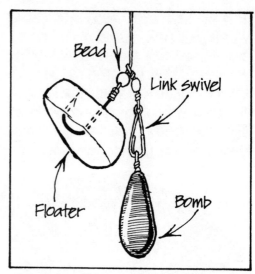

Weighted floater rig before casting

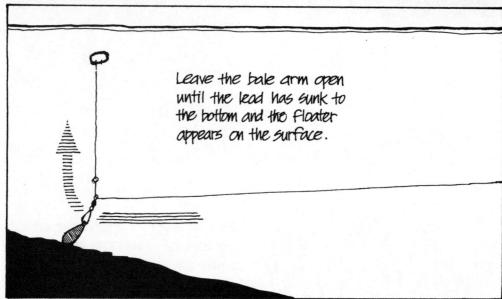

Leave the bale arm open until the lead has sunk to the bottom and the floater appears on the surface.

Engage the bale arm, reel in any slack line and place the rod in rests. A monkey climb indicator will be easier on the eyes than straining to see a floater away in the distance. The addition of an electronic indicator will also be a help if attention wanders a little.

The bait should now be floating in a typical carp patrol route.

If the carp ignore the floating bait a turn on the reel handle will position the bait just below the surface. This ruse often works.

Where steeply-shelving banks drop suddenly into very deep water a floating weight will be needed to assist the casting of a small floating bait. Quarries, for instance, are invariably surrounded by dense tree growth, necessitating the use of an underarm cast. The extreme depth often found in such waters would negate the practicality of the previous rig, as the drawing shows.

Far too much excess line to make this method practical.

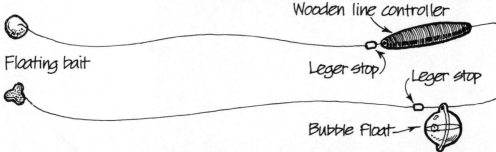

Wooden line controller

Floating bait

Leger stop

Leger stop

Bubble float

Either of these rigs will allow controlled casting in a restricted area.

Cast here to avoid spooking fish.

Reel back very slowly to fish the bait here. With snags so close it pays to hold the rod all the time.

Once a fish has been hooked, full side-strain should be applied to turn it away from underwater snags created by the tree branches.

IF a hooked carp is allowed too much free rein it may kite around the tree with disastrous consequences.

Play out a hooked carp in this area.

Flooded quarry pits are potentially dangerous places. Depths of 90-100ft (27-30m) can occur directly beneath an angling position. Wearing a strong pair of ankle length boots is a sensible precaution to combat the steep, uneven banks, and waders should never be worn. Always fish with a companion in such places, and have a length of rope in the tackle bag, just in case of an accident.

Legering

This is the most commonly practised method of taking common, mirror or leather carp. It is generally a waiting game with long periods of inactivity between runs. Fishing with two rods at the same time will, going by the law of averages, increase the angler's chances of getting to grips with a fish. However, this does not always hold true, as there is no substitute for fishing in the right place at the right time. One carefully placed bait will always outfish two, cast indiscriminately.

So therefore it pays to spend some time on a reconnaissance of the water to be fished. Living close to the water will, of course, allow the fortunate angler much more opportunity to do this than an angler who has to travel some distance and whose time is limited. What are we looking for though? We are looking for areas where, for one reason or another, carp tend to congregate, feed or regularly pass through. Any such area can then be groundbaited in preparation for the introduction of the hookbait. The presence of the groundbait, laced with free hookbait samples will stimulate the carp to feed in a confident manner.

Although long casts, in the more heavily fished waters, are usually associated with legering, close-in legering can also be effective, provided that the right precautions are taken. When close-in legering, always keep a low profile; avoid heavy foot-falls on the bank, and sudden movements—even a hand raised too high will spook a carp which is just about to suck in a bait. Loud talking, too, can be heard at close range under water. Close-in legering should be approached and carried out with the same attitude as one would adopt for stalking carp.

Warm wind

B

Weed and scum

A

The illustration above shows an ideal situation for trying out some close-in leger fishing. The angler could fish anywhere from point A to B, but most experienced anglers would opt for point A — directly facing the wind.

The next step would be to introduce a few handfuls of hookbait samples. These might be easier to introduce from point B — using the assistance of the wind. As a freelined rig would cause less disturbance, in what would in all probability be fairly shallow water, the hookbait would need to have enough weight in itself to make a short cast into the wind possible. In this instance then, luncheon meat would seem to be the most practical choice.

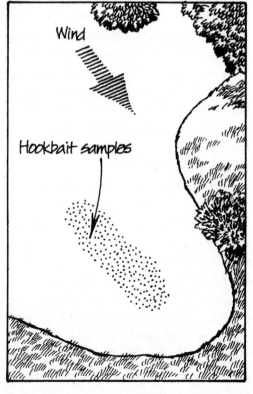

Wind

Hookbait samples

However, the wind may be too strong to allow any freelined bait to be cast, and a small lead may have to be used.

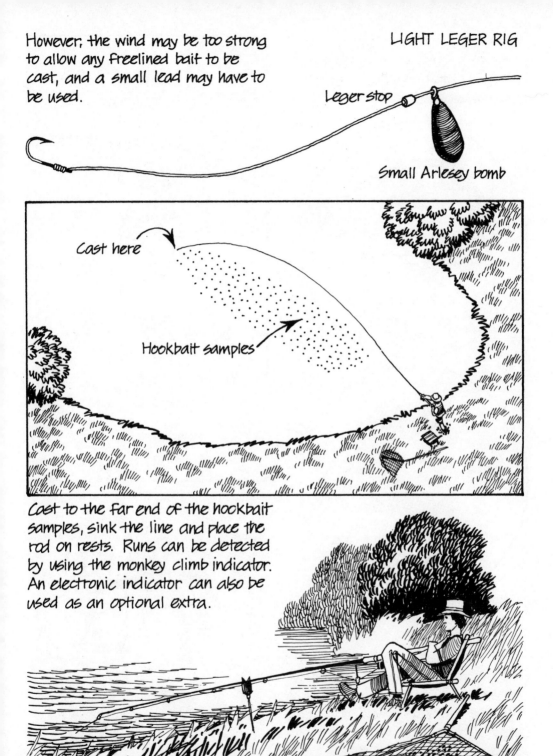

Leger stop

Small Arlesey bomb

Cast here

Hookbait samples

Cast to the far end of the hookbait samples, sink the line and place the rod on rests. Runs can be detected by using the monkey climb indicator. An electronic indicator can also be used as an optional extra.

55

When adjusting a monkey climb indicator leave enough space beneath the 'monkey' to register drop-back bites.

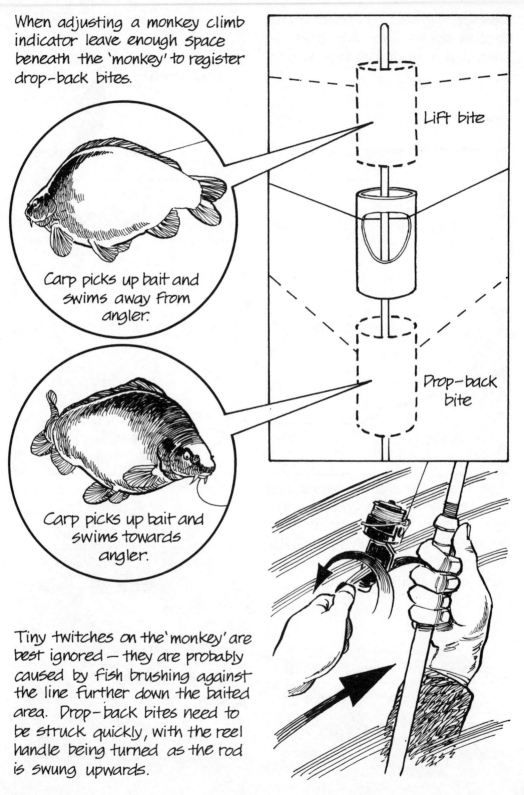

Lift bite

Drop-back bite

Carp picks up bait and swims away from angler.

Carp picks up bait and swims towards angler.

Tiny twitches on the 'monkey' are best ignored — they are probably caused by fish brushing against the line further down the baited area. Drop-back bites need to be struck quickly, with the reel handle being turned as the rod is swung upwards.

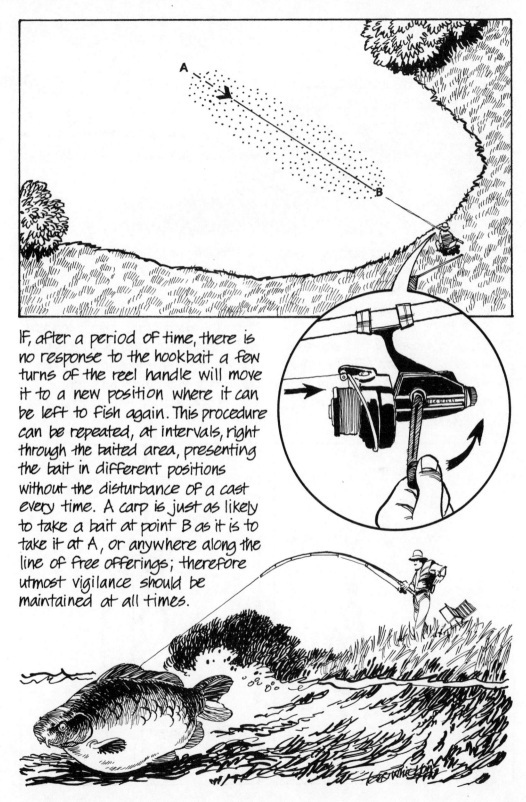

IF, after a period of time, there is no response to the hookbait a few turns of the reel handle will move it to a new position where it can be left to fish again. This procedure can be repeated, at intervals, right through the baited area, presenting the bait in different positions without the disturbance of a cast every time. A carp is just as likely to take a bait at point B as it is to take it at A, or anywhere along the line of free offerings; therefore utmost vigilance should be maintained at all times.

Long-range legering

On many hard-fished waters where the carp tend to retreat to areas well away from the bank, casts of up to 100yds (91m) are often needed in order to reach the fish.

To produce a cast of this distance, a lead of about 2oz(60g) in weight will have to be used, coupled with a rod which has a test curve of 2lb (0·90 kg).

A sensible precaution, in order to eliminate snap-offs, is to tie a length of shock leader line between the hook length and the main line. Prior to casting, the shock leader will occupy the reel spool for about six turns. The main line should be about 8lb (3·05 kg) test — the shock leader about 15lb (7kg.)

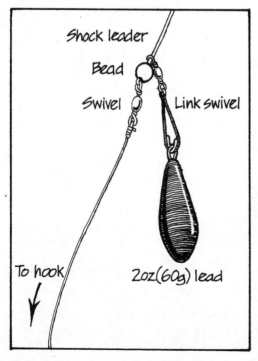

Shock leader
Bead
Swivel
Link swivel
To hook
2oz(60g) lead

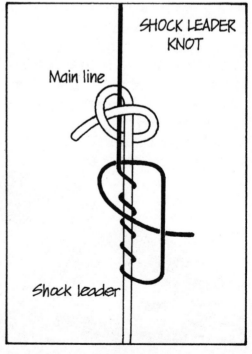

SHOCK LEADER KNOT

Main line

Shock leader

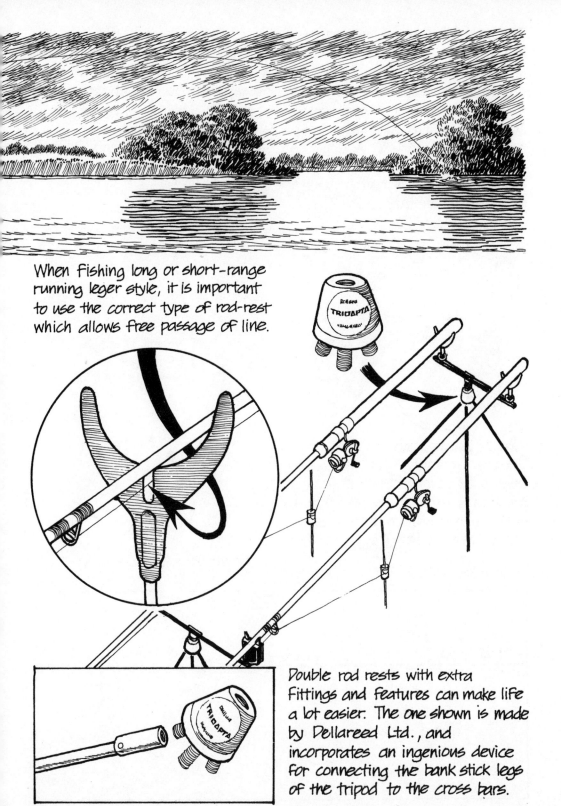

When fishing long or short-range running leger style, it is important to use the correct type of rod-rest which allows free passage of line.

Double rod rests with extra fittings and features can make life a lot easier. The one shown is made by Dellareed Ltd., and incorporates an ingenious device for connecting the bank stick legs of the tripod to the cross bars.

The need for accuracy when ground-baiting and casting is of paramount importance when long range fishing. The hookbait should come to rest in the pre-baited area, looking exactly like one of the free offerings lying on the bed of the lake. A very strong catapult will be needed to hurl balls of groundbait or boilies the required distance.

Particle baits such as beans and sweetcorn pose a bit of a problem as they are so light, and their range, if fired from a catapult, would be limited. However, by using a gadget called a 'Doppleganger' small particles can be cast many yards with accuracy.

Type of catapult suitable for long distance groundbaiting. The cup will have to be taken from a standard groundbait catapult as this particular model is sold with a narrow leather pouch, intended for firing metal balls.

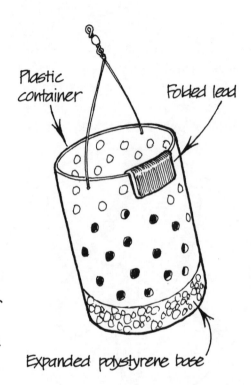

Plastic container

Folded lead

Expanded polystyrene base

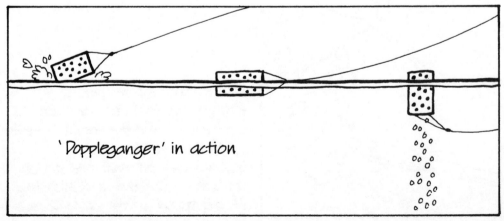

'Doppleganger' in action

The advantage of using two rods is that two baits can be fished, at the same time, in two different areas, thus improving the chances of a run. It is advisable, however, to have a generous angle between the two lines in order to minimise the risk of a tangle if a hooked carp gets out of control. Better still, have a companion who can reel in the spare line until the fish has been brought to the net.

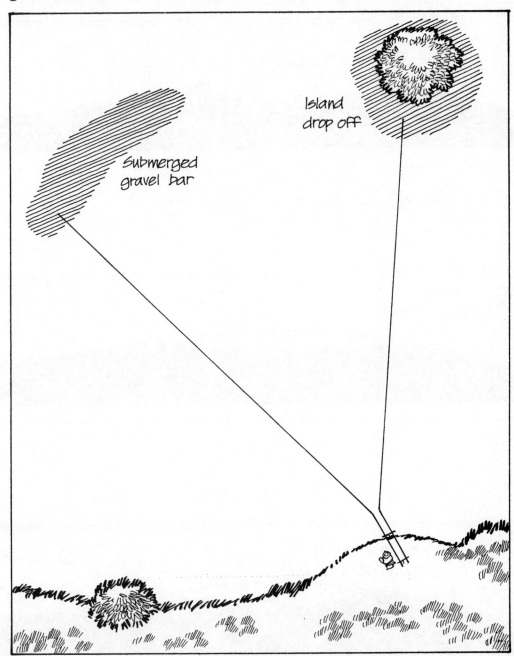

Casting a leger

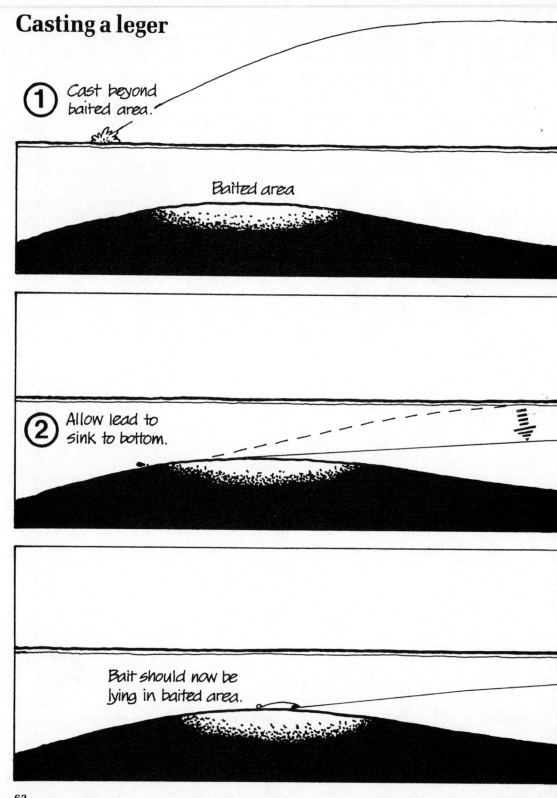

1 Cast beyond baited area.

Baited area

2 Allow lead to sink to bottom.

Bait should now be lying in baited area.

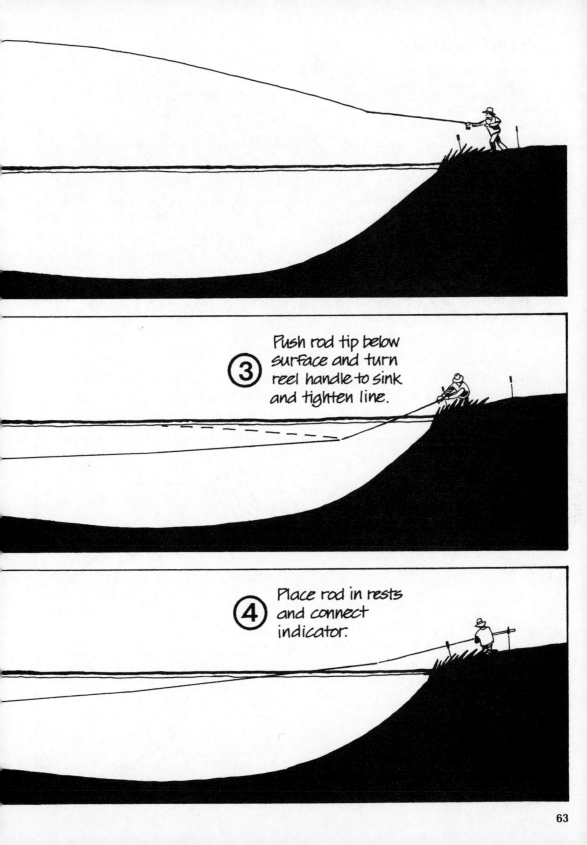

③ Push rod tip below surface and turn reel handle to sink and tighten line.

④ Place rod in rests and connect indicator.

Night fishing

Fishing after dark should be approached in a positive and well organised manner. The selected pitch should be one which has been fished previously, during daylight. Tackle should be arranged, before nightfall, in such a way that it is easily located in the dark.

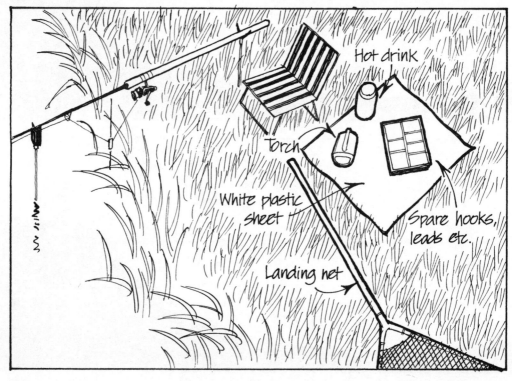

Hot drink

Torch

White plastic sheet

Landing net

Spare hooks, leads etc.

It is seldom so dark at night that far-bank features cannot be used as an aid to consistently accurate casting to a baited area.

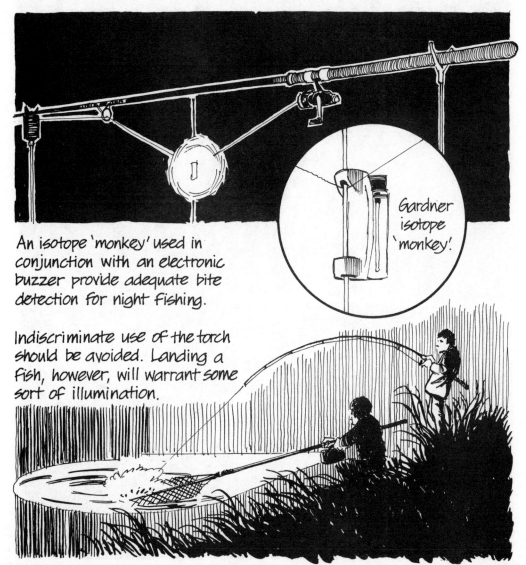

Gardner isotope 'monkey'!

An isotope 'monkey' used in conjunction with an electronic buzzer provide adequate bite detection for night fishing.

Indiscriminate use of the torch should be avoided. Landing a fish, however, will warrant some sort of illumination.

Margin fishing

A very effective method during the hours of darkness and early in the morning, during summer.

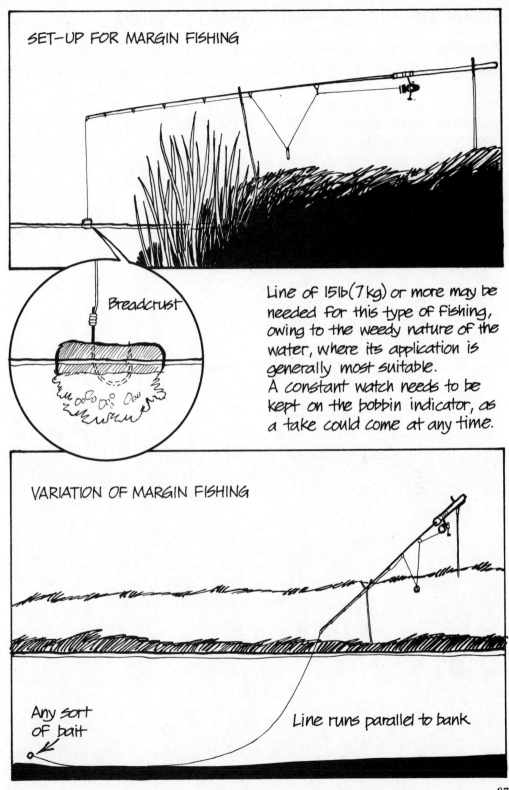

SET-UP FOR MARGIN FISHING

Breadcrust

Line of 15lb (7kg) or more may be needed for this type of fishing, owing to the weedy nature of the water, where its application is generally most suitable.
A constant watch needs to be kept on the bobbin indicator, as a take could come at any time.

VARIATION OF MARGIN FISHING

Any sort of bait

Line runs parallel to bank

Hooking, playing and landing a carp

When the rising indicator or the buzzer signals a run, the rod should be held in the horizontal position. The bale arm on the reel should be in the closed position. When the line draws tight the rod should be swung up and back, over the right shoulder. The index finger is now on the reel spool and the other hand is holding the reel handle.

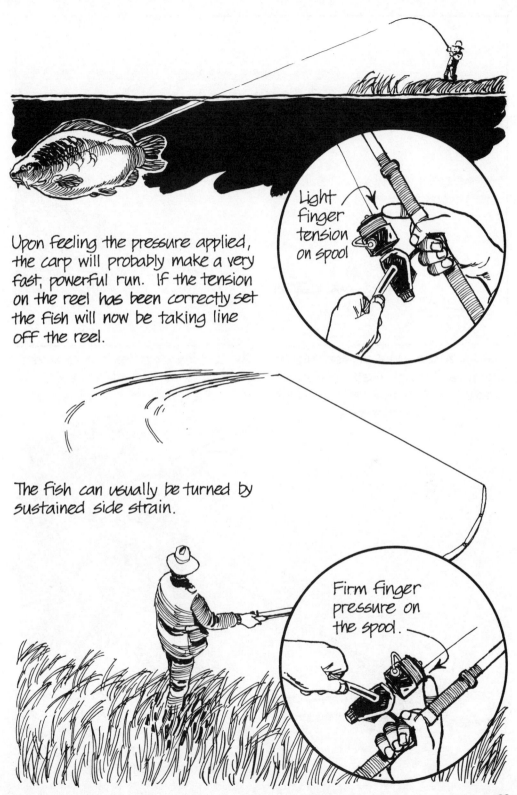

Upon feeling the pressure applied, the carp will probably make a very fast, powerful run. If the tension on the reel has been correctly set the fish will now be taking line off the reel.

Light finger tension on spool

The fish can usually be turned by sustained side strain.

Firm finger pressure on the spool.

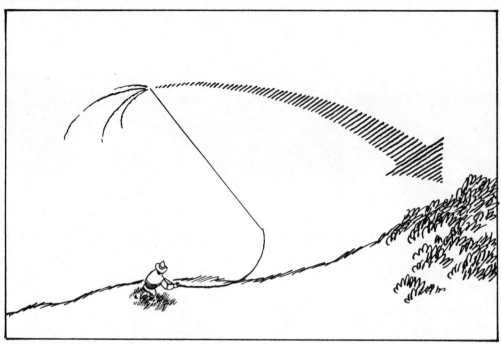

Sidestrain can cause a phenomenon known as 'kiting', when the fish swings back towards the near bank.

One can imagine the consequences if the bank is liberally endowed with thick vegetation and snags.

When the fish tires and turns on to its side, submerge the net and guide the fish towards it. Keep the net stationary until the fish is within the frame area.

Lift the frame of the net clear of
the water and put down the rod.

Grasp the net in both hands,
beneath the frame, and lift.

Carry the fish clear of the water and place the net and the fish on a soft base of grass or moss.

The hook can then be removed with a disgorger or forceps.

Avoid using disgorgers with this sort of tip. The points could cause damage to the mouth of the fish, resulting in an untimely death.

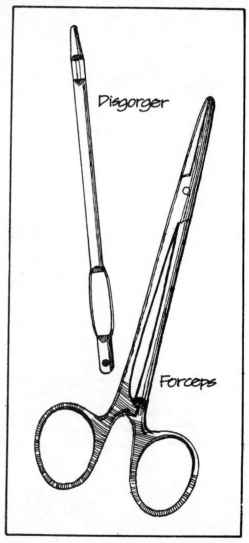

Disgorger

Forceps

Winter carp

Not so long ago it was generally considered a waste of time to pursue carp during winter. Now, it is considered a viable proposition, and many stout-hearted souls venture forth, even when snow is lying on the banks. Milder spells obviously provide the best chances when a bait can be presented in the deeper areas of water.

Weighing a carp

The first requirement for this procedure is a knotless mesh bag or sling. This is saturated with water to prevent removal of protective slime from the fish. Place the sling on a soft base of grass or moss and gently place the fish on the mesh.

Always make sure that your hands are wet when handling a fish.

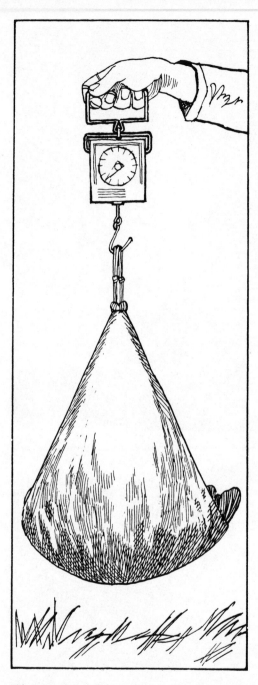

Weighed in this manner the carp will lie quietly until the procedure is complete. It can then be returned carefully to the water.

Never weigh a live fish in this manner — it will damage the delicate gill filaments.

Before weighing or photographing, the carp can be kept in a keepsack. Keepnets are not suitable for large carp. The sack can be staked out in the margins where the carp will lie quietly until it is released. The considerate angler will not leave a carp in a sack for a long period of time.

Carp should be returned by holding the fish upright in the water until it swims away of its own accord.

Accessories

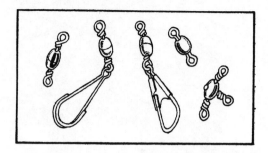

SWIVELS AND LINK SWIVELS:
Used in the construction of
leger rigs.

FLOAT RUBBERS: Available in a
large variety of sizes, either cut
to size, or in tube form which
allows the angler to tailor his own.

NAIL CLIPPERS:
The ideal tool for trimming the
tag end of a knot.

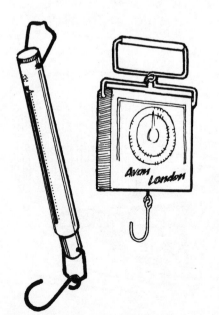

SPRING BALANCE / SCALES:
Good quality spring balances
and scales are costly items, but
the accuracy and long service they
provide, if well looked after, will
more than compensate for the
initial outlay.

POLAROID SUNGLASSES :
These glasses eliminate glare,
enabling the angler to see fish
which are swimming beneath the
surface of the water.

ARLESEY BOMBS : A selection of
these invaluable leads is a must
in the carp fisher's armoury.
Sizes from 2½oz(70g) to ½oz
(15g) should cover all contingencies.

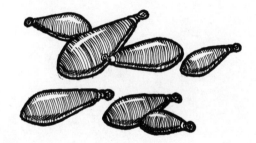

SPARE REEL SPOOLS:
All fixed-spool reels have spools
which are detachable and easily
changed in a matter of seconds.
Be prepared for all eventualities
by having a collection of spools,
each loaded with a different
breaking strain line.

UMBRELLA:
This invaluable item should be
included in every carp angler's
list of equipment. For the night
fisherman it is doubly valuable,
as it provides the base support
for the brolly camp.

BROLLY CAMP

Useful knots

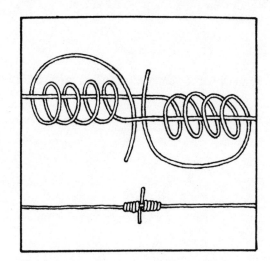

BLOOD KNOT: The only knot for joining two lengths of equal diameter monofilament which provides a neat and strong joint.

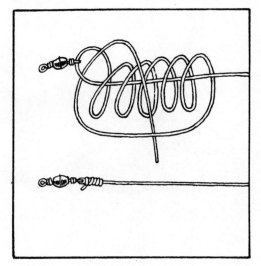

TUCKED HALF-BLOOD KNOT: An improvement on the plain half blood knot, and one that should be employed regularly when fishing for strong heavy-weight fish such as carp.

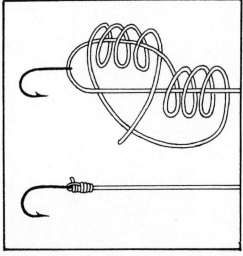

GRINNER KNOT: This knot is equally as good, if not better, than the tucked half blood knot. It just will not come adrift. Always moisten the line with saliva before tightening any knot. Never jerk the line tight. A firm steady pull is sufficient. Leave about 1/32 in (1mm) of tag protruding from the finished knot.